D1052811

AMERICAN TYCOONS

Other titles in the **Collective Biographies** *series*

Collective Biographies

AMERICAN TYCOONS

Carl R. Green and
William R. Sanford

Enslow Publishers, Inc.

40 Industrial Road	PO Box 38
Box 398	Aldershot
Berkeley Heights, NJ 07922	Hants GU12 6BP
USA	UK

http://www.enslow.com

Library of Congress Cataloging-in-Publication Data

Green, Carl R.
    American tycoons / Carl R. Green and William R. Sanford.
       p. cm. — (Collective biographies)
    Includes bibliographical references and index.
    Summary: Describes the lives of ten very different business people
spanning America's history from the Civil War to the Computer Age,
including Cornelius Vanderbilt, Bill Gates, Henry Ford, Louis Burton
Mayer, and Madame C.J. Walker.
    ISBN 0-7660-1112-7
    1. Businesspeople—United States—Biography—Juvenile literature.
[1. Businesspeople.] I. Sanford, William R. (William Reynolds),
1927–   . II. Title. III. Series.
HC102.5.A2G73   1999
338.092'273
[B]—DC21   98-50786
                                               CIP

Printed in the United States of America

10 9 8 7 6 5 4 3 2 1

To Our Readers:
All Internet addresses in this book were active and appropriate when we went to press.
Any comments or suggestions can be sent by e-mail to Comments@enslow.com or to
the address on the back cover.

Illustration Credits:
A'Lelia Bundles/Walker Family Collection, p. 60; AP/Wide World Photos,
p. 88; Courtesy Library of Congress, Reproduced from the *Dictionary of
American Portraits*, published by Dover Publications, Inc., in 1967, p. 32;
Johnson Publishing Co., Inc., p. 78; *Los Angeles Times* Photo, Ken Lubas,
p. 67; Microsoft Corporation, pp. 96, 104; Reproduced from the
Collections of the Library of Congress, pp. 10, 19, 22, 29, 38, 42, 46, 50,
70, 74, 91; Underwood Photo Archives, S.F., p. 55; USC News Service/Irene
Fertik, p. 86.

Cover Illustration: Microsoft Corporation

Contents

Preface

Turn back the clock about three centuries. In that long-ago time most people lived and worked on the land. Families depended on farm animals and on their own muscle power to raise crops, make tools, and weave cloth. Most people lived and died within a few miles of their birthplace. Townsfolk and city dwellers bought from small shops the goods they could not make for themselves. The great landowners enjoyed immense wealth and boundless power. They relished their noble titles and scorned those who made and sold products.

All that changed in the 1700s with the dawn of the Industrial Revolution. As steam engines replaced manual labor, power passed into the hands of bankers, merchants, and factory owners. Craftsmen and farmworkers moved to fast-growing cities to find work. A few did well, but most worked for pennies an hour and lived in disease-ridden slums. Factory owners ignored the plight of their workers and hired women and children at even lower wages. Plant managers fired the few brave souls who protested sweatshop conditions.

In the early 1800s, the Industrial Revolution spread from Europe to the United States. The growth of the factory system created golden opportunities for the nation's entrepreneurs. These were the risk-takers who organized and operated large business ventures. By the early 1900s, newspaper reporters were referring to the top-ranked entrepreneurs as *tycoons*. The word seemed to fit, because it came from the Japanese *shogun*, "an all-powerful military ruler." One of the first American tycoons was Cornelius Vanderbilt. After building a shipping empire, Vanderbilt turned to land transportation. His canal boats and trains brought coal to factories, delivered finished goods, and helped open the western frontier.

As the demand for steel increased, Andrew Carnegie merged a number of small mills into a steel-making giant. Financial wizards such as John Pierpont Morgan built their own empires by arranging the financing for million-dollar deals. Like steel, the oil industry was badly fragmented until John D. Rockefeller took matters in hand. Under his leadership, Standard Oil emerged as a symbol for industrial power. Henry Ford joined the ranks of the nation's tycoons by marketing the cheap, dependable Model T car. In addition to putting America on wheels, Ford changed factory work by introducing the moving assembly line.

In a very different field, Madame C.J. Walker reigned as the nation's first African-American woman millionaire. Madame Walker built her empire by producing and selling a popular line of cosmetics. In Hollywood, Louis B. Mayer was richly rewarded for helping turn America into a nation of moviegoers. His Metro-Goldwyn-Mayer Studio produced some of the most popular films ever made.

In our own time, the Industrial Revolution has given way to the Information Age. Ever since Johannes Gutenberg invented printing from movable type in the 1400s, the world's appetite for information has been growing. In this century, John H. Johnson took advantage of the demand by bringing a new family of magazines into America's homes. The key invention of the Information Age was the digital computer. A Chinese immigrant named An Wang made his fortune with inventions that led to faster, more efficient computers. Bill Gates became a tycoon by designing and marketing the software programs that allow the rest of us to use and enjoy computers.

These ten tycoons all created great fortunes, but money was not the true measure of their success. History remembers them because they built enterprises that changed the way people live, work, travel, and amuse themselves.

Cornelius Vanderbilt (1794–1877)

1

Cornelius Vanderbilt

Transportation Tycoon

In 1863, steamship tycoon Cornelius Vanderbilt set his sights on the New York and Harlem Railroad. The line was losing money, but it was the only railroad that ran into New York City from the north and east. Vanderbilt bought enough shares at eight dollars apiece to gain control. Then he began to upgrade the Harlem Railroad. The sixty-nine-year-old millionaire, his friends chuckled, had a new toy. They stopped laughing when the line's stock rose to fifty dollars a share. Flying high now, Vanderbilt talked the city into granting him the right to lay track down Broadway. The stock soared to one hundred dollars.

At that point Daniel Drew jumped into the battle. Drew, a bitter rival from Vanderbilt's days as a shipping tycoon, urged members of the city council to sell the stock short. Those who agreed to the scheme first borrowed New York and Harlem shares from their stockbrokers. Then they sold them to the public. They planned to buy the shares back later when the price fell, repay the brokers, and pocket a quick profit. To make sure the price of the shares did fall, the council canceled the New York and Harlem's right-of-way.

News of the scheme soon reached Vanderbilt. Quickly, he propped up share prices by buying the stock the plotters were selling short. By summer's end, shares were selling for $180. The councilmen had no choice but to give Vanderbilt what he wanted. First they restored the right-of-way, then they begged him to sell them the stock they owed their brokers. Drew wrote a jingle to describe the trap Vanderbilt had set: "He that sells what isn't his'n, must pay up or go to prison."[1]

At the last minute Vanderbilt sold the plotters the stock they needed. Thanks to his tough stand, he was $5 million richer.

Starting Out

The Vanderbilt family story begins around 1650. That was when Jan Aertsen van de Bildt left Holland and settled on New York's Staten Island. A few generations later, on May 27, 1794, Cornelius Vanderbilt was born on the family farm. The baby was named for his father, who marketed his crops across the bay in Manhattan. The elder Vanderbilt's frequent absences saddled his wife Phebe with the twin tasks of managing the farm and raising the children.

At age eleven Cornelius rebelled against further schooling. His parents shrugged and put him to work. Given a chance to sail his father's flat-bottomed, two-masted boat, Cornelius quickly mastered Upper New York Bay's currents, tides, and winds. Soon he was ferrying loads of produce, hay, and fish to Manhattan Island.

Five years later, Cornelius announced that he was planning to run away to sea. Rather than argue, Phebe struck a shrewd deal with her son. If he would clear and plant a rocky eight-acre field, she would loan him one hundred dollars to buy his own boat. The blue-eyed, six-foot teenager rounded up some friends and went to work. When the job was done, Phebe handed Cornelius the one hundred dollars she kept hidden in the grandfather clock. He used the money to buy the *Swiftsure* and start a ferry business. Within a year, he ferried enough passengers (18¢ one way, 25¢ for a round-trip) to repay the loan and to pocket a one thousand dollar profit.[2]

During the War of 1812, Cornelius hauled workmen and supplies to forts around the bay. He also carried food to the blockaded city from farms along the Hudson River. Those who knew him agreed that he was tough, fearless, and trustworthy. In December 1813, he stopped work long enough to marry his teenage cousin, Sophia Johnson. But by the next morning the ambitious nineteen-year-old was back on the docks.

Fame and Fortune

When peace returned, Cornelius Vanderbilt put his profits to work. Before long his ships were carrying oysters, whale oil, and other products between Chesapeake Bay and New York. By the time he turned twenty-seven in 1818, he had saved nine thousand dollars. That was a small fortune in an age when skilled workers earned two dollars a day. His home life prospered, too. In the course of a forty-five-year marriage, Sophia gave birth to thirteen sons and daughters.

By this time Robert Fulton's first steamboats were chugging across the harbor. Fulton was able to talk the state into granting him a monopoly on New York's steamboat traffic. Vanderbilt wanted a piece of the action, so he sold his sailing ships and cut a deal with Thomas Gibbons to build a steam ferry. To fill the *Bellona's* seats, Vanderbilt and Gibbons reduced the fare between New York and New Jersey from four dollars to one dollar. They made up the losses by overcharging for food and drink.

Fulton's monopoly had passed into the hands of Aaron Ogden. Because each trip broke the law, Vanderbilt had to hide in a secret closet in the *Bellona's* hull whenever the police came to arrest him. At last the rival shipper, Ogden, tired of the game and took Gibbons to court. The case went to the

United States Supreme Court, which gave Gibbons and Vanderbilt a landmark victory in 1824. In the case known as *Gibbons* v. *Ogden,* the court ruled that only Congress can regulate the movement of goods between states.[3]

By 1830, Vanderbilt had expanded again. New Yorkers began their trips by crossing the Hudson on his ferries. Then they jounced across New Jersey in his stagecoaches and sailed down the Delaware River to Philadelphia on his steamboats. Unable to match Vanderbilt's low fares, rival shippers joined forces and paid him not to compete on their routes. Vanderbilt pocketed the payoff and shifted his operations to the Hudson Valley. To fill his seats, he sometimes passed out free tickets. This time, worried competitors paid him one hundred thousand dollars to withdraw. Vanderbilt used the cash to buy more steamboats and enter new markets. By the mid-1840s "Commodore" Vanderbilt's fleet was sailing as far north as Boston and as far south as Cuba.

After gold was found in California in 1848, Vanderbilt pioneered a fast, cheap route from the East Coast to the goldfields. His ships sailed down the San Juan River to Lake Nicaragua, a passage that cut six hundred miles off the disease-ridden route across Panama. In 1858, rival shipping lines counted their losses and offered Vanderbilt $672,000 a year to shut down the Nicaragua route. The Commodore took the money and invested it in a transatlantic steamship business. His flagship, the *Vanderbilt,* was hailed as the largest ship afloat. The iron-hulled vessel crossed from New York to England in the record time of nine days, one hour.

Tall and thin, with a square jaw and a strong nose, the Commodore cut a fine figure; however, neither looks nor wealth could buy him a place in high society. New York's bluebloods laughed at his old-fashioned clothes, his profane speech, and his bad grammar. When he dined out, he sometimes offended his hosts by spitting tobacco juice on their rugs. Vanderbilt shrugged off the snubs, returned to Staten Island, and built a fine mansion on the old family farm.

Vanderbilt jumped into railroading with his 1863 victory over Daniel Drew. A year later he began buying stock in the Hudson River Railroad. Drew, spoiling for revenge, talked state legislators into another short selling scheme. The plan would work, Drew said, if the state kept Vanderbilt from combining the New York and Harlem with the Hudson. Vanderbilt kept his nerve, bought up all the Hudson stock, and watched his holdings triple in value. Drew, beaten again, lost a million dollars. Some legislators went broke.

Vanderbilt extended his tracks to Albany, where he built a two-thousand-foot-long bridge across the Hudson. In 1866, rivals gained control of the New York Central Railroad, which served the region west of Albany. When the new owners closed their tracks to Vanderbilt's westbound freight, he closed his bridge to their trains. This forced the Central's passengers to walk two miles through the snow to catch their connecting trains. Faced with empty seats and freight piling up in Albany, the Central opened its tracks to Vanderbilt's trains. Within two years, the Commodore's railroad system stretched from New York to Chicago.

In 1868, Vanderbilt bought stock in Daniel Drew's Erie Railroad, a line that linked New York City with the Midwest. Rather than share control with his old rival, Drew flooded the market with Erie stock. The new stock reduced the value of Vanderbilt's shares and enriched Drew and his partners. Vanderbilt hit back with a court ruling that ordered Drew not to issue more Erie stock. Drew fled to New Jersey, where he bribed the legislature to approve the stock issue. His partner Jim Fisk sneered, "If this printing press don't break down, I'll . . . give the old hog all he wants of Erie."[4] In the end, Drew and Fisk allowed Vanderbilt to walk away, but only after he had lost $1.5 million. For the richest man in America, the loss did more harm to his pride than to his bank account.

The Bottom Line

Critics called Cornelius Vanderbilt a pirate in business clothes. Yet even his enemies agreed that he was hardworking, intelligent, fiercely competitive, and a man of his word. Faced with choices that involved millions of dollars, Vanderbilt always seemed to make the right decisions. Perhaps it helped that he took more pleasure in making money than in spending it.

At home, Vanderbilt did not pretend to be a loving husband and father. To "cure" second son Cornelius Jeremiah of gambling, Vanderbilt called in the police. Eldest son William endured a long series of harsh tongue-lashings. When his wife, Sophia, refused to move to New York City, the Commodore locked her in an insane asylum until she changed her mind. After Sophia died of a stroke in 1858, Vanderbilt married the young Frances "Frank" Crawford.

True to his frugal nature, Vanderbilt gave little money to charity. Frank, who knew how to manage her aging husband, did talk him into giving fifty thousand dollars to New York's Church of the Strangers. Late in life, he dug deeper and gave $1 million to help build Central University in Nashville. By the time the school opened, it had changed its name to Vanderbilt University.

Vanderbilt died of cancer on January 4, 1877. After a modest funeral, the reading of his will sent shock waves through the family. Out of an estate of $100 million, the Commodore left his widow only $500,000 and their New York townhouse. His daughters received $2.45 million—to be divided eight ways. Black sheep Cornelius Jeremiah picked up the income from a $200,000 trust fund. Everything else went to patient, hardworking William.

Central University in Nashville, Tennessee, changed its name to Vanderbilt University after the era's richest tycoon donated a million dollars to its building fund.

The Commodore built a one hundred dollar loan into one of the world's great fortunes. What kind of man was he? "What do I care about the law?" he once said. "Hain't I got the power?" On another occasion he remarked, "I have been insane on the subject of money-making all my life."[5]

2

Andrew Carnegie

Steel Tycoon

Andrew Carnegie could be ruthless, but he had a social conscience, too. It was the duty of the rich, he said, to use their money to help people. In pursuit of that goal, he followed three rules:

1. *Don't spoil your heirs.* Giving money to one's children, Carnegie believed, was the same as placing a curse on them.

2. *Give with warm hands.* Giving only counts, he said, if you're generous while you're alive. Most men leave money to charity in their wills, he argued, because they can't take it with them.

3. *Help those willing to help themselves.* Carnegie said he would rather throw his money away than encourage "the slothful, the drunken, [and] the unworthy."[1]

Andrew Carnegie (1835–1919)

In pursuit of those goals, Carnegie paid for the building of 2,811 town libraries. In the early 1900s, ordering a Carnegie library was a simple three-step process. *Step one:* the town sent its request to Carnegie's New York home. *Step two:* the town provided a site near the town center. *Step three:* the town promised to support the library with an annual budget equal to 10 percent of Carnegie's gift. Construction began when Carnegie's check arrived (a sum equal to two dollars per resident).

Newspapers kept a running box score as others caught the giving spirit. One of Carnegie's chief rivals was oil tycoon John D. Rockefeller. In 1913, *The New York Herald* reported that Carnegie was an easy winner—$332 million to Rockefeller's $175 million.[2] That's more than $3 billion in today's dollars!

Starting Out

Andrew was born to Will and Margaret Carnegie on November 25, 1835, in Dunfermline, Scotland. Will was a skilled weaver, but power-driven looms were stealing work from hand-craftsmen. In 1848, eager to make a fresh start, the family sailed for America and settled in Pittsburgh, Pennsylvania. To earn a living, Will wove tablecloths and Margaret sewed shoes.

Thirteen-year-old Andrew loved school, but the family needed money. A textile mill put the boy to work in a smelly basement, where he sealed the grain of wooden bobbins by dipping them in oil. The pay was $1.20 a week. When the chance came, Andrew switched to a better job tending a furnace. His boss was impressed by his penmanship and promoted him to clerk. After working his long shifts, Andrew trudged off to night classes to learn accounting.

In 1849, a job as a telegraph office messenger opened. Andrew loved the work and soon taught himself to read Morse code. Promoted to operator at twenty dollars per month, he began learning how to do business American style. He wrote to a friend, "In Scotland, I would have been a poor weaver all my days. But here surely I can do something better."[3] Will Carnegie died in 1855, leaving twenty-year-old Andrew as the head of the family.

He stood only five feet three inches tall, but young Carnegie impressed all who met him. Tom Scott, a superintendent on the Pennsylvania Railroad, hired him as his personal telegrapher. Carnegie's hard work paid off in 1859 when Scott moved up to vice-president. Andrew stepped into Scott's job as superintendent at a yearly salary of fifteen hundred dollars. The new manager proved to be very good at cutting costs and improving operations. Each well-planned move turned a tidy profit for the railroad.

His future looked secure, but Carnegie was restless. When the time was ripe, he told himself, he would quit and pursue a career as an investor.

Fame and Fortune

Investors make money by buying and selling everything from bushels of wheat to entire companies. A wise investment, Carnegie knew, could earn more in a year than a factory worker earned in a lifetime. Poor investments, of course, could ruin you just as quickly.

Carnegie took his first plunge in 1856. He borrowed five hundred dollars and bought ten shares of Adams Express Company stock. The gamble paid off. As the company prospered, management paid shareholders a dividend of a dollar per month for each share they owned. If Carnegie had any doubts about becoming an investor, the first ten-dollar check erased them.

His big break came when inventor Theodore Woodruff showed him his new railroad sleeping car. Carnegie jumped at the chance to buy a one-eighth interest in the company. He borrowed $217.50 to make the first payment and arranged to pay the balance in installments. Sleeping cars sold briskly, and by 1860 Carnegie's investment was bringing in five thousand dollars a year. "Blessed be the man who invented sleep," he joked.[4]

One success led to another. Carnegie and William Coleman paid forty thousand dollars for some promising lots after oil was discovered north of Pittsburgh in 1859. When drillers brought in a gusher, the value of the land soared to $5 million.

Carnegie used his profits to buy shares in more companies. Whatever he touched seemed to turn to gold. An $11,000 investment in an oil firm returned $17,868 in the first year.

In 1861, the outbreak of the Civil War put his plans on hold. Tom Scott, now the assistant secretary of war, picked Carnegie to manage the Union army's telegraph and railroad systems. The new manager's first big test came when Confederate forces cut the railroad that linked Baltimore and Washington. Moving quickly, Carnegie organized repair crews and reopened the line. By summer, the North's hopes for a quick victory were fading, and the Pennsylvania Railroad recalled Carnegie to his regular duties. Three years later, the Union army sent him a draft notice. Convinced that he had done his duty, Carnegie paid a young man $850 to take his place. This was legal at the time—and $550 more than the law required.

Carnegie often saw schedules disrupted by collapsing wooden bridges. The mishaps convinced him that the bridges of the future would be made of iron. While the war still raged, he rounded up several partners and founded the Keystone Bridge Company. He borrowed $1,250 to pay for his one-fifth share—and earned six times that amount the next year.

By 1865, Carnegie was making more money from investments than he made in salary. He quit the railroad and traveled through Europe for nine months. On his return, refreshed in body and spirit, he went shopping for solid, well-managed companies. "You'll never find me in speculation," he promised.[5] When owners and managers quarreled, Carnegie often stepped in as peacemaker.

In 1868, Carnegie thought about retiring, then decided that he was having too much fun.[6] An 1872 visit to England, where he saw the new Bessemer steelmaking process, convinced him that the future lay in steel. Three years later Carnegie opened his own steel mill, the J. Edgar Thomson Steel Works.

Carnegie's goal was to control every stage of production. Because steel mills burn coal, which first must be processed into hot-burning coke, he bought into Henry Clay Frick's coke company. By 1881, Carnegie owned half the company. The partners often clashed over labor policy. Unlike Frick, Carnegie wanted to treat workers fairly. He never forgot the days when he made his living by working with his hands.

In 1886, Carnegie was saddened by the deaths of his mother and brother. A year later, after a turbulent courtship, he married Louise Whitfield. Their only child, Margaret, was born in 1897. Carnegie, a father for the first time at sixty-two, built Skibo Castle in Scotland for his wife and daughter. With an income of $25 million a year, he could afford the luxury.

Carnegie was relaxing in Scotland in 1892 when a bloody strike broke out at his Homestead Works. Frick locked out the strikers and hired guards to patrol the plant. Shooting broke out, and the state militia had to be called in. With Carnegie's approval, Frick brought in strikebreakers to work the mill. Carnegie did not feel that this harsh action broke his vow to treat the working man fairly. In his view, union members who went on strike had given up their right to his respect.

The white-haired tycoon still had a few tricks up his sleeve. In 1899, he merged all his companies into the giant Carnegie Steel Company. Then came a major surprise. In 1901 he sold Carnegie Steel to J.P. Morgan for $480 million.

The Bottom Line

The public was amazed when Carnegie sold out. The grizzled old millionaire explained that he was moving on to a new phase of his life. In his role as a philanthropist, he had donated libraries to towns and organs to churches. Now he set out to promote world peace, advance science, and improve schools. To make sure the funds were given wisely, he set up institutions known as foundations. In the years since his death, these foundations have given away more than $2 billion. Carnegie dollars support projects that range from mapping DNA to helping television shows such as Sesame Street stay on the air. Of all the good works, the Carnegie Hero Fund may have been his favorite. Carnegie liked to hand out medals to every-day heroes who "preserve and rescue their fellows."[7]

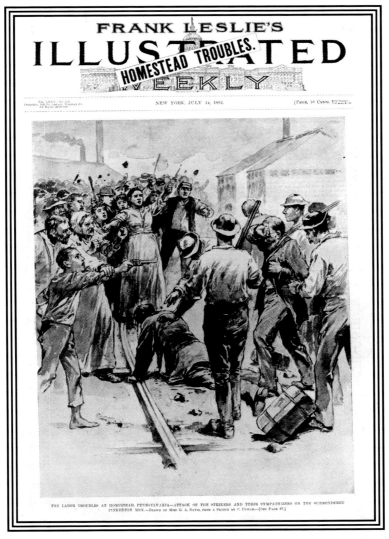

This scene from the cover of *Illustrated Weekly* pictures the outbreak of fighting between the Pinkerton guards and the strikers at Carnegie's Homestead Works.

Carnegie never forgot the hard work and shrewd investments that made his gifts possible. A high point of his life was his triumphant return to his birthplace in Dunfermline in 1881. With his mother at his side, he rode through the town's streets, waving to cheering crowds. To mark the happy occasion, Carnegie gave the town a new library.

For all his wealth, Carnegie remained open and alert to the end. He counted prime ministers, presidents, and philosophers—along with everyday people—as friends. In April 1919, he watched with pride as his daughter married a young engineer. A few months later, on August 11, he died peacefully in his sleep.

His death reminded friends of an article Carnegie wrote in 1889. In "The Gospel of Wealth" he warned, "The man who dies rich dies disgraced."[8] Andrew Carnegie spent his last years making sure that no one would say that about him.

3

John Pierpont (J.P.) Morgan

Financial Tycoon

The year was 1902 and the stage was set for a clash of titans. On one side stood Theodore Roosevelt, president of the United States. On the other stood the tycoon known as the most powerful man in America, John Pierpont Morgan.

The conflict grew out of Morgan's habit of gobbling up rival railroads. In 1901, he had set out to end the cutthroat competition his Northern Pacific Railroad faced from rival lines. First, he formed an alliance with Jim Hill's Great Northern. Then, he outbid E. H. Harriman for the Burlington Railroad. To protect his growing monopoly from competition, he set up the Northern Securities Company. The new holding company controlled all three lines.

John Pierpont (J.P.) Morgan (1837–1913)

Morgan was not worried that he was violating the Sherman Antitrust Act. The 1890 law made it illegal for companies to interfere with the free flow of trade between the states, but business had never felt the law's sting. Now newly elected Theodore Roosevelt was vowing to wage war against "the tyranny of . . . wealth."[1]

In February 1902, word leaked out that the government was about to file an antitrust suit against Northern Securities. Morgan took a train to Washington. At a White House meeting, he complained that Roosevelt should have consulted him. "If we have done anything wrong," he snapped, "send your man [the attorney general] to my man [my lawyer] and they can fix it up."[2]

Roosevelt refused to "fix things up." The antitrust case went to trial, where the Supreme Court ruled against Northern Securities. Morgan's defeat marked the end of an age in which powerful financiers ruled entire industries.

In 1909, his two terms finished, Roosevelt sailed for Africa to hunt big game. On hearing the news, Morgan said he hoped that "the first lion he meets does [its] duty."[3]

Starting Out

John Pierpont Morgan was born April 17, 1837, in Hartford, Connecticut. His father, Junius Morgan, was one of the nation's largest dry-goods merchants. The family called the baby Pip and despaired over his poor health. He almost died twice—once while cutting teeth and a month later from convulsions.

Pip's childhood illnesses often kept him out of school. At last his health improved enough to allow him to attend Boston's English High School. Then, at age fifteen, a bout with rheumatic fever almost crippled him. Hoping a warm climate would help, Junius sent Pip to the Azores islands, located west of the coast of Portugal. Sun and exercise soon worked a small miracle. The boy's weight shot up, and he regained his strength. In the years that followed, he grew to a robust six feet and 210 pounds.

In 1854, Junius was working in London as a partner in George Peabody's banking firm. Encouraged by his son's recovery, Junius sent him to school in Switzerland. Only the onset of a severe case of acne marred the teenager's stay there. It was the first round in a lifelong struggle with the disfiguring skin condition.

From Switzerland, Pip moved on to Göttingen University in Germany. The nineteen-year-old excelled in math and enjoyed a lively social life. At twenty, however, he felt ready to launch his business career. He returned to New York and signed on with Duncan, Sherman, a firm that served as agent for London-based bankers. In his new job, he began a thirty-year custom of sending his father a twice-weekly report.

In 1859, Pip landed in New Orleans on a business trip. In a daring gamble, he used company funds to buy a shipload of coffee. Although he resold the coffee at a profit, his rash action alarmed his bosses. Denied a partnership, Pip left the firm. Before long, he found work as the American agent for Peabody's London firm.

Fame and Fortune

The outbreak of the Civil War in 1861 left John Pierpont Morgan with some hard choices. The chance of making money on the war won out over his religious and patriotic beliefs. Morgan bankrolled a gun dealer who bought five thousand old smoothbore carbines for $3.50 each. After gunsmiths rifled the barrels to make them more accurate, the dealer resold the guns to the Union army. The sales price of $22 per rifle gave Morgan a quick $6,500 profit. Two years later he received his draft notice. As was the custom with wealthy men, he escaped service by paying another man to take his place.

In the fall of 1861, still youthfully romantic, Morgan married Mimi Sturgis, though she was ill. After the wedding, the couple left on a honeymoon cruise. The North African sun was no match for Mimi's tuberculosis, and she died four months later. J.P., as friends called him, fought his grief by plunging into his work. In 1864, Junius Morgan set up the firm of Dabney, Morgan and installed J.P. as the junior partner. Before long the young man was taking home fifty thousand dollars a year.

In 1865, Morgan took time off to marry Fanny Tracy. In the years that followed, Fanny gave birth to three daughters and a son, John Pierpont, Jr. (nicknamed Jack). J.P. filled the family's New York home with treasures purchased on his trips abroad. In 1872, he bought a country retreat that overlooked the Hudson.

When war broke out between France and Germany in 1870, Morgan arranged a daring $50 million loan to the French government. The action showed that his company had become a powerful force in world banking circles. Back home, Morgan proved that he had a talent for merging and rebuilding struggling companies. Under his steady hand, the money-losers soon turned around. His firm, now known as Drexel, Morgan & Company, was becoming one of New York's leading banking houses.

Success did little to improve Morgan's health. At times he suffered from fainting spells and severe headaches. His acne flared up and turned his nose a bright red. During the 1870s, he sought relief by sailing off to foreign lands. His favorite destination was Egypt, where he sailed up the Nile with his family. On each of his trips he bought shiploads of ancient treasures.

In 1885, Morgan moved into railroading. His first step was to merge the New York Central with several competing lines. Within three years, he had added railroads in Pennsylvania and Ohio. It annoyed him that smaller lines sometimes lowered their rates to attract customers. Despite the 1887 Interstate Commerce Act, Morgan tried to talk the heads of the major railroads into agreeing to fix rates. The railroad men refused. They knew that rate-fixing would create a firestorm of public protest.

Morgan cared little for public opinion or the law. In a telling exchange, his lawyer once told J.P. that what he wanted to do was illegal. Morgan replied, "That is not what I asked you. I asked you to tell me how it could be done legally. Come back tomorrow or the next day and tell me how it can be done."[4]

Junius Morgan was killed in a carriage accident in April 1890. After a period of mourning, J.P., now fifty-three, used some of his inheritance to buy a new yacht—the 204-foot *Corsair II.* Anthony Drexel, Morgan's partner, died three years later. Free to pursue his own projects, J.P. took control of several major railroads whose price had fallen when the national economy nose-dived during the panic of 1893. The mergers reduced competition—and led to his 1902 battle with President Roosevelt.

In 1895, the public worried that the nation's paper money was losing its value. To protect their savings, people were demanding that the United States Treasury redeem their paper money for gold. The run on the nation's gold reserves gave Morgan a chance to be a hero. To show faith in the economy, he organized a syndicate that bought $62 million in United States bonds. The Treasury then used the money to build up its gold reserves. The near-panic faded away—and Morgan banked a profit of about three hundred thousand dollars.

Convinced that bigger was better, Morgan bought out Andrew Carnegie's steel empire for $480 million. Years later, Carnegie told Morgan he had thought of asking for $580 million. Morgan puffed his big cigar and said that he would not have quibbled over an extra $100 million.[5] By then he had combined a number of steel plants into United States Steel. The company was the nation's first billion-dollar corporation.

J.P. Morgan, famed for his ill temper, could be quite pleasant when he was relaxing on his yacht. In this photo from 1903, a bodyguard escorts Morgan (left) from the dock to a waiting carriage.

Stories of Morgan's immense wealth and power did not sit well with the public. Humorist Finley Peter Dunne put a comic spin on those sour feelings. He imagined that Morgan had called in one of his bank presidents: "'James, . . . take some change . . . an' r-run out an' buy Europe f'r me,' [Morgan] says. 'I intind [sic] to re-organize it an' put it on a paying basis.'"[6]

The Bottom Line

Like his fellow tycoons, Morgan was a study in contrasts. At work, he ruled his domain with an iron hand. One observer compared his fierce stare to being caught in the headlamp of a locomotive. Out in public, his son-in-law observed, he "barged along as if he had been the only man" on the street.[7] In fits of temper, he sometimes threw food at servants who displeased him. When newspapers charged him with plotting to take control of the country, Morgan refused to comment on the rumors. "I owe the public nothing!" he thundered.[8]

At home, Morgan could be a charming host. He was fond of children and took pride in showing off his art collection. When he traveled or entertained, it was on a royal scale. To Fanny's despair, he sometimes left her at home while he entertained beautiful women on his yacht. For all his rudeness and disregard of public opinion, however, Morgan called himself a religious man. He often walked to St.

George's Episcopalian Church, where he knelt and sang hymns by the hour.

At age seventy-two Morgan was wearing out. In January 1913, he fell ill while traveling on the Nile. During a stopover in Rome, he lost the power of speech and then fell into a coma. On March 31, the mighty J.P. Morgan died in his suite at the Grand Hotel. His son Jack stepped forward to take command of the House of Morgan.

Writers of that era ignored J.P.'s sins when they summed up the tycoon's life. A biographer called him the "mightiest personal force in American business life." The *New York World* went an admiring step further. The paper described Morgan as standing "bestride the world like a Colossus."[9]

4

John D. Rockefeller

Petroleum Tycoon

In 1870, companies were going broke and workers were losing their jobs. However, John D. Rockefeller saw an opportunity in the growing demand for oil. He gathered some partners and launched Standard Oil. Although the million-dollar company controlled 10 percent of the nation's oil business, profits lagged.

Rockefeller blamed the hard times on cutthroat competition. In 1871, he conspired with friendly oil refiners and the major railroads to form the South Improvement Company. As the scheme took shape, the members announced freight charges of $2.80 a barrel for oil shipped from Cleveland to New York. What nonmember refiners did not know was that the railroads had agreed to a secret deal. For every barrel,

John D. Rockefeller (1839–1937)

the railroads returned $1.80 of the $2.80 charge to South Improvement's refiners. The railroads further sweetened the pot by paying the refiners another $1.80 from the $2.80 a barrel paid by nonmembers.[1]

With the under-the-table agreement in his pocket, Rockefeller stalked his rivals. They had two choices, he told them. They could sell out to him, taking payment in Standard Oil stock—or they could fight and go broke. Three months later, news of the scheme leaked out. Oil producers promptly shut down their pumps, a move that cut off South Improvement's refiners from their supplies of crude oil. Then, as public outrage grew, the state of Pennsylvania revoked South Improvement's charter.

Although his railroad allies deserted him, Rockefeller refused to be beaten. By the time South Improvement collapsed, Standard Oil controlled a quarter of the country's refineries. Rockefeller was well on his way to building a great industrial empire.

Starting Out

John Davison Rockefeller was born July 8, 1839, in a small house near Richford, New York. William and Eliza Rockefeller were far from rich. William sold cancer cures for twenty-five dollars a treatment and speculated in land. With her husband away for months at a time, Eliza raised their five children to be like her—religious, disciplined, and frugal. As a twelve-year-old, John made fifty dollars by hoeing fields and selling turkeys. Instead of spending the money, he loaned it to a farmer at 7 percent interest. Years later he explained, "I determined to make money work for me."[2]

The family moved to Cleveland in 1853, where John attended high school. He excelled in math and debating. In 1855, John finished his formal schooling and moved on to Folsom's Commercial College. His ten-week business course taught him the basics of accounting and bookkeeping. At home his father showed him how to draw up loans and other legal papers.

In September 1855, John went looking for a job. After weeks of searching, he landed a job as an assistant bookkeeper at Hewitt and Tuttle. His employers, who bought and sold products on commission, offered the teenager four dollars a week. John could have made more money elsewhere, but he wanted business experience. From that day on, he proved to be careful, honest, and persistent. Except for church, his life revolved around the office.

Within the year, John was keeping the books, arranging deals, and collecting debts. People called him "Mr. Rockefeller," although he was still a teenager. A photo of John from this time shows a narrow, serious face and conservative clothes. The famous iron nerve shows in his strong, direct gaze.

Fame and Fortune

In 1859, Rockefeller quit his job after his boss ignored his request for a raise. He then talked fellow clerk Maurice Clark into joining him in a commission business. Trade was brisk, and the partners prospered. Patient and careful about details, Rockefeller bargained shrewdly and kept his temper in check.

When the Civil War began in 1861, Rockefeller stayed home and tended to business. The Union was buying mountains of food and supplies, and the money rolled in. Rockefeller, however, could see change coming. The railroads were laying new tracks, and farm shipments heading east soon would bypass Cleveland. A more secure future, he judged, lay in shipping refined petroleum products. In 1863, partnered with Clark and with a refiner named Samuel Andrews, he launched an oil business. To cut costs, Rockefeller purchased and stored crude oil when prices were low. He also built a larger refinery and bought out one of his largest rivals.

Rockefeller took time out in 1864 to marry Laura Spelman. It turned out to be a close and loving marriage. Laura enriched her husband's life by bringing art and culture into their home. She also gave birth to four daughters and a son—and corrected his sometimes shaky spelling. "Without her keen advice," Rockefeller said later, "I would be a poor man."[3]

In 1865, Rockefeller bought out Clark's share of the oil business for $72,500. Firmly in charge, he increased profits by stressing self-sufficiency. His firm did its own plumbing, made its own barrels from its own trees, and hauled oil in its own wagons.

In this 1861 photo, workers drill for oil near Titusville, Pennsylvania. John D. Rockefeller refined and shipped petroleum products made from the oil that flowed from fields like this one.

His workers shipped kerosene, paraffin, lubricants, and other products. The refinery also produced gasoline, although there was little demand.

Henry Flagler, a wealthy businessman, signed on as a partner in 1867 and became one of Rockefeller's closest friends. The partners plowed profits back into the company and borrowed to build a second refinery. Eager to tap foreign markets, Rockefeller sent his brother William to New York to open an office. In 1870, Rockefeller shuffled his holdings into a company he named Standard Oil. At thirty, he reigned over the world's largest oil business.

Along with a love of hard work, Rockefeller brought a fresh, creative mind to business. He studied every detail and forgot nothing. Bankers trusted him and helped him survive setbacks by signing off on huge loans. When his partners quarreled, Rockefeller often stepped in to keep the peace. He kept workers happy by paying good wages, but he could be ruthless if they dared go on strike.

By the end of the 1870s, Standard Oil was refining 90 percent of the nation's oil. From his base in Ohio, Rockefeller expanded into New York, Pennsylvania, West Virginia, and Kentucky. To cut transport costs, he built his own pipelines and bought others. He also hammered out rebate agreements with several major railroads. These sweetheart deals meant that Standard Oil paid only eighty cents a barrel to ship its oil. Smaller companies paid almost twice as much.

In 1882, Rockefeller tightened his control by setting up the Standard Oil Trust. He saw the trust as a tool for forcing rivals to join him or perish. His handpicked board of trustees managed the trust's vast holdings and hired its managers. The trust reigned supreme until 1892, when an Ohio court dissolved it. Many of the trust's companies then joined hands with Rockefeller to form Standard Oil Company of New Jersey. The new giant controlled three fourths of the nation's oil business.

During the 1880s Rockefeller moved his family to New York. By the 1890s, however, the stress of managing his empire was wearing him down. Almost overnight, it seemed, he began to look his age—or older. His face was lined, he had trouble sleeping, and he suffered from stomach disorders.

For a time, Rockefeller tried to keep up the pace. He bought iron ore deposits, a railroad to carry the ore, and a fleet of lake steamers. More and more, his immense wealth weighed on him. In 1891, he hired Frederick Gates to manage his fortune. Five years later he stopped going to the office. In 1897, at age fifty-eight, John D. Rockefeller retired to his country home. It was time to give his money away, he said.

The Bottom Line

Even when he worked for four dollars a week, Rockefeller gave to his church and to good causes. Now the problem lay in finding ways to give away a fortune that in 1912 reached $900 million. With Gates doing his legwork and with Andrew Carnegie as his model, the oil tycoon began the task of setting up charitable foundations. Some of his money funded the Rockefeller Sanitation Commission, which wiped out a hookworm epidemic in the rural South. Another $80 million went to the University of Chicago. Over $180 million flowed into the Rockefeller Foundation, which still funds state-of-the-art scientific research.

As he aged, Rockefeller took delight in his grandchildren, golf, and a gentler public image. Making peace with the public was a long-postponed task. For years, most Americans had believed that the Rockefeller fortune was based on shady deals and dishonest business practices. To counter that bad feeling, the old man took to handing out dimes to people in the street. The small gesture made him seem almost lovable.

Rockefeller ate little, but he still played golf. During the winter his family sent servants ahead to remove snow from the course. As a ninety-year-old, the old tycoon shrank to less than a hundred pounds. He was staying in Ormond Beach, Florida, when he died on May 23, 1937, at age ninety-seven.

Thanks to his father's scientific giving, John Junior inherited "only" $500 million. The old tycoon also left giant footprints. Standard Oil furnished the oil and gas that fueled the nation's growth. His foundations continue to finance useful research. Rockefeller's thirst for power, on the other hand, led to antitrust laws that controlled runaway monopolies like Standard Oil. During his heyday, a newspaper dubbed Rockefeller "the richest man in America." He declined the honor. "If I have no other achievement to my credit than the accumulation of wealth," he said, "then I have made a poor success of my life."[4]

Henry Ford (1863–1947)

Henry Ford

Automobile Tycoon

The year was 1901, and the automobile was in its infancy. A budding Detroit carmaker named Henry Ford thought he could attract customers by winning an auto race. Starting almost from scratch, Ford and a team of five craftsmen built a two-cylinder, twenty-six horsepower racer. The engine boasted two sparking devices that a local dentist had coated with porcelain. They were the world's first spark plugs.

A crowd of eight thousand race fans gathered at the Detroit Fairgrounds on October 10. Alexander Winton's forty horsepower race car was the favorite in the ten-mile main event. His speedy racer had been clocked at a world record of forty-eight miles per hour for the mile. By race time a series of breakdowns had eliminated all but Winton and Ford. Ford drove his racer himself. Spider Huff, his partner, crouched on the running board to add balance on turns.

Winton took the lead, his tires kicking up dirt that peppered Ford's face. After three laps around the one-mile track, Ford fell three hundred yards behind. Then he made his move. He cut the corners more sharply and gained on the straightaways. By lap six, he had closed the gap. At that point the lead car began to smoke and lose power. Ford passed Winton on lap seven and kept the lead to the end. The crowd cheered when his time was announced at 13:23.8—an average speed of 43.5 miles per hour.[1]

The race's sponsors never did award the one thousand dollar prize. Ford hardly noticed, because he had won a far greater prize. The young engineer had proved that he could build fast, durable cars. All across the country people were talking about this new carmaker.

Starting Out

Henry Ford was born July 30, 1863, near Dearborn, Michigan. William and Mary Ford were amazed to see their oldest son develop into a self-taught mechanic. As a boy, Henry repaired his neighbors' watches. If he needed a new tool, he made it himself.

When he was sixteen, Henry walked to Detroit and signed on as an apprentice at a machine shop. A few months later he moved on to the Detroit Drydock Company, where he could work on engines. By 1882, he was a full-fledged machinist.

The Westinghouse Engine Company hired him to demonstrate its steam engines to farmers.

During this time Henry built his first working engine, a tiny steam turbine that he hooked up to a lathe. He also found time to court pretty Clara Bryant, and in 1888, he married her. William Ford gave the couple a forty-acre farm. Henry built a house for his bride, and his parents hoped he was ready to settle down. Instead, he hatched a plan to build a horseless carriage.

The new dream meant packing up and moving to Detroit. The couple's only child, Edsel, was born there in 1893. As chief engineer of the Edison Illuminating Company, Henry was on call night and day. He spent his free time in his tiny workshop. The long hours paid off in 1896 when he drove his four-horsepower Quadricycle over Detroit's bumpy streets.

In 1899, Henry joined the Detroit Automobile Company. The firm produced only a few cars before closing its doors. Buoyed by his 1901 racing success, Henry then organized the Henry Ford Company. A year later he resigned after bankers opposed his plans to build a new racing car.

Undaunted, Ford raised $28,000 and in 1903 he organized the Ford Motor Company. That same year, he rolled out his first car and christened it the Model A.

Fame and Fortune

The 1903 Model A was powered by a two-cylinder engine that produced eight horsepower. The car buzzed along at thirty miles an hour—but buyers complained of its overheating, oil leaks, faulty brakes, and other problems. One by one, Ford solved the problems with improved designs and better-quality parts. Outside the workshop, he fought off a lawsuit that accused him of infringing on patents held by rival automakers.

In 1908, Ford put everything he had learned into a new car, the Model T. The car's four-cylinder engine was dependable. And its high clearance conquered the mud and ruts of rural roads. Best of all, the "Tin Lizzie" was easy to drive and repair. In 1909, a Model T survived quicksand, fire, mud, and snow to win a cross-country race from New York to Seattle. The time was an astounding twenty-two days, fifty-five minutes. To meet the mounting demand for the car, Ford built a new plant in Highland Park. Visitors gawked at its many windows and dubbed it the Crystal Palace.

Ford liked to say, "Time loves to be wasted."[2] In 1913, he cut back on that waste by designing the first assembly line. On the line, moving belts carried partially built cars past the workers. Each worker performed a single task, using parts stored at the workstation. As the number of worker-hours per car fell from more than twelve to slightly under two, the price of the 1913 Model T dropped to $440. The profits from skyrocketing sales made Ford a very rich man.

In 1914, Ford hit on a plan to improve the morale of workers who disliked assembly-line jobs. In a daring move, he doubled the average worker's pay from $2.50 a day to $5.00 a day. He also reduced the plant's ten-hour shifts to eight hours. By the next day newspapers were proclaiming, "God Bless Henry Ford!"[3] Ten thousand job seekers lined up outside the plant. Ford said he hoped the pay raise would let his workers buy the cars they worked so hard to build.

At fifty, Ford was still lean and youthful-looking. Only his graying hair and the lines around his mouth

When Prince Nicolas of Romania visited him, Henry Ford (right) gave his guest a personal tour of the Highland Park assembly lines.

hinted of age and overwork. With Clara and Edsel he was a loving husband and father, but at the plant Ford sometimes played cruel jokes. One of his favorites was to catch a worker chewing tobacco, which was against the rules. When that happened, Ford would slip up behind the man and clap him hard enough on the back to make him swallow his plug of tobacco. Then he would laugh wildly as the man got sick. James Couzens said that his friend Ford was really two people. One was generous and caring, the other was arrogant and self-centered.[4]

In 1914, Germany plunged Europe into the chaos of World War I by attacking France. Soon the other European nations had joined in the fighting. Ford hated violence in all its forms. He condemned the war and any attempt to involve the United States in the fighting. Convinced by antiwar activists that the two sides wanted to end the fighting, he chartered a ship to carry peace envoys to Norway. The peace talks opened late in 1915, but the warring countries paid little heed. Ailing and discouraged, Ford gave up and sailed for home.

In 1920, Ford used a $75 million loan to buy out his major stockholders. He relished his role as sole owner, but sales were slow. Although the Tin Lizzie's price dropped as low as $240, the Model T was losing its appeal. General Motors took over as the nation's number one carmaker with the stylish new Chevrolet. In 1927, Ford reluctantly approved the changeover to an updated Model A. The car featured a stick shift, shock absorbers, a safety windshield, and a quiet ride. Edsel Ford, who had taken over as company president in 1919, designed the stylish body.

Sales dipped again after the collapse of the stock market ushered in the Great Depression of the 1930s. As the ranks of the jobless rose, car sales dropped. To make matters worse, in Ford's view, workers were lining up to join labor unions. "The average man won't really do a day's work unless he . . . cannot get out of it," he complained.[5]

In 1937, General Motors and Chrysler broke ranks and signed union contracts. Ford held out, certain that his well-paid workers would never unionize. When union organizers appeared, he hired security guards to drive them off. In the end, 97 percent of the company's workers voted to join the union. Faced with those numbers, Ford signed a contract with the United Auto Workers in 1941.

Edsel was in charge, but Ford could not let go. Time after time he interfered with his son's attempts to modernize. The company stumbled badly, and by 1940 its market share had fallen to one car in five. To compound the old man's misery, Edsel died of cancer in 1943. "I never believed that anything like this could happen to me," the grieving father said.[6] He took back the title of president and held his old job through the remaining years of World War II. In 1945, after suffering two strokes, he turned the job over to his grandson, Henry Ford II.

The great auto tycoon died quietly on April 7, 1947. More than one hundred thousand mourners filed past his coffin as his body lay in state at the Henry Ford Museum.

The Bottom Line

Henry Ford was neither sinner nor saint. Despite some personal failings, he gave Americans the gift of cheap, dependable transportation. Like his idol, the inventor Thomas Edison, he was a gifted engineer who could analyze and solve tough problems. Ford could be stubborn, too, as in this much-quoted statement about the Model T: "A customer can have a car painted any color he wants so long as it is black."[7]

In all, 15 million black Model T's rolled off Ford's lines between 1908 and 1927. That was the longest run of any model until the Volkswagen Beetle came along. Of equal importance to the modern industrial age was Ford's obsession with cutting waste. His assembly lines ushered in the age of mass-produced consumer goods.

Ford once said, "History is more or less bunk. . . . The only history that is worth a tinker's damn is the history we make today."[8] Despite that harsh judgment, he spent millions to preserve the story of his era. The Henry Ford Museum and Greenfield Village in Dearborn, Michigan, show visitors a glimpse of a past that might have been lost.

When all is said and done, Henry Ford is one of the giants who put the world on wheels. As nations battle smog and traffic jams, that gift has turned out to be a mixed blessing. It was humorist Will Rogers who foresaw our dilemma. "It will take a hundred years to tell whether [Ford] helped us or hurt us," Rogers said, "but he certainly didn't leave us where he found us."[9]

Madame C.J. Walker (1867–1919)

6

Madame C.J. Walker

Cosmetics Tycoon

Life looked bleak for Sarah Breedlove in 1904. Her husband was dead, and her daughter, Lelia, was away at college. To support herself and Lelia, the African-American woman worked as a cook and laundress. Then, as if being poor was not burden enough, her hair began to fall out.

Breedlove prayed for help. Later, she told friends that the answer came to her in a dream. "In that dream," she said, "a big black man appeared to me and told me what to mix up for my hair. Some of the remedy was grown in Africa, but I sent for it, mixed it, put it on my scalp, and in a few weeks my hair was coming in faster than it had ever fallen out."[1]

When friends saw the results, they asked for samples of the amazing hair grower. Soon they were telling their friends that their thin, dry hair was growing in long and healthy. No longer did they feel compelled to remove kinks by pressing their hair with hot flatirons. Breedlove began selling her Wonderful Hair Grower as fast as she could mix it. To guard against copycats, she kept the formula secret.

A new world was opening for Sarah Breedlove. Her parents had lived and died in the cotton fields of Louisiana. Now, a small miracle had taken place. The struggling laundress (soon to marry and become Madame C.J. Walker) had taken the first steps toward launching a successful business.

Starting Out

Sarah Breedlove was born December 23, 1867, in a dirt-floored shack on a plantation in northeast Louisiana. Her parents, Owen and Minerva Breedlove, were ex-slaves who worked as sharecroppers. Sarah toiled beside them in the cotton fields until both died of yellow fever. After the funeral, seven-year-old Sarah went to live with her sister, Louvenia, in Vicksburg, Mississippi.

Moving to the city did not end the hard times. Sarah's work as a laundress left little time for schooling. At age fourteen, eager to escape the beatings handed out by Louvenia's husband, she married Moses McWilliams. Her daughter, Lelia, was born two years later. In 1887, Moses died at the hands of a lynch mob. His death left his wife and two-year-old daughter to fend for themselves. Hoping for a better future in a big city, Sarah moved north to St. Louis.

Sarah was a good worker, but most doors were closed to her. For eighteen years, from 1887 to 1905, she supported herself and Lelia by washing clothes for white families. Somehow, long hours and an income of $1.50 a week did not make her bitter. Sarah did charity work and worshipped at St. Paul's African Methodist Episcopal Church. Unable to read and write, she made sure that her daughter stayed in school. Later, she scrimped and saved so Lelia could attend Knoxville College.

It was during this time that Sarah's hair began to fall out. Like many other African-American women of her day, she had tried a number of hair care treatments. She did not know that her hair loss had been caused by poor diet, stress, and the chemicals found in some hair treatments. She mixed up her own hair grower—and soon her friends and a widening circle of customers were clamoring to buy it.

Fame and Fortune

By 1905, Sarah had married and divorced a second husband. When news came that her brother had died, she joined her sister-in-law and four nieces in Denver. With only $1.50 in her pocket, she started her own business. Work as a maid paid the bills, and at night she mixed her hair grower in a washtub. On her days off she went door-to-door, showing women how to use her product.

Six months later Sarah married Charles J. Walker, a newspaper sales agent. Walker used his marketing skills to help build his wife's business. Sarah celebrated her step up in social class by calling herself Madame C.J. Walker. In time, the business drove the couple apart. Charles wanted to play it safe, but Madame Walker was determined to build a cosmetics empire. After the couple divorced in 1912, Walker stayed on as a sales agent. His wife kept her new name.

Madame C.J. added new products and promoted the Walker System. Clients washed their hair with her shampoo, rubbed in the hair grower, brushed vigorously, and applied heated combs. As demand grew, Madame C.J. hired women to sell her products. Walker agents soon showed up in towns and cities across America. The women made their calls dressed in white shirtwaists tucked into long black skirts. The Wonderful Hair Grower and sixteen other beauty products came in packages that featured Madame C.J.'s portrait. The sharecropper's daughter became one of the nation's best-known African-American women.

Madame C.J. traveled throughout the South and the East. At each stop she gave lectures and demonstrations in homes, clubs, and churches. In 1908, she opened a training school in Pittsburgh and named it the Lelia Beauty College in honor of her daughter.

Lelia, who had run the mail-order business and trained "hair culturists" back in Denver, took charge of the school. The graduates agreed to sell only Madame C.J.'s products and use only her methods. In an age when hygiene was mostly ignored, they also promised to practice "cleanliness and loveliness."

Critics argued that Madame C.J. harmed African-American pride by encouraging her clients to straighten their hair. Madame C.J. tackled the issue head-on. She said, "Let me correct the erroneous impression held by some that I claim to straighten hair. I want the great masses of my people to take greater pride in their personal appearance and to give their hair proper attention."[2]

In 1910, Madame C.J. moved her headquarters to Indianapolis. There she built a five-story plant to produce her beauty products. The sprawling building also housed a Greek-style theater, lunchroom, drugstore, beauty parlor, and private offices. Madame C.J. reigned as the sole owner of the Madame C.J. Walker Manufacturing Company. The enterprise employed some three thousand workers. At its peak, about twenty thousand Walker agents were active in the United States, Central America, and the Caribbean.

Reporters described Madame C.J. as America's first self-made female millionaire. The cosmetics tycoon followed Lelia east to New York City in 1914 and built a limestone townhouse on West 136th Street. Lelia (who changed her name to A'Lelia when she married in 1918) later made the house a gathering place for talented African-American artists, musicians, and authors. In 1917, Madame C.J. built a $250,000 country house, which she called Villa Lewaro. She spent another $500,000 to furnish the home. Guests marveled at a 24-carat gold-plated piano, a $15,000 pipe organ, Persian rugs, and fine oil paintings.

Eager to make up for her lack of schooling, Madame C.J. hired tutors to teach her to read and write. Her handwriting improved, and she took pleasure in reading good books. Added leisure also gave her time for good causes. She gave freely to the National Association for the Advancement of Colored People (NAACP) and its antilynching campaign. The YMCA, YWCA, African-American women's clubs, and African-American educational groups also drew her support.

A lifetime of hard work took its toll on Madame C.J.'s health. Doctors told her to relax, that her blood pressure was too high. Madame C.J. shrugged and kept on with her busy schedule. After falling ill in St. Louis, she was forced to return to New York. She died there on May 25, 1919, of kidney failure. After funeral services at her villa, she was buried in Woodlawn Cemetery in the Bronx, New York.

A'Lelia inherited the bulk of her mother's estate. A second provision of the will, however, attracted widespread comment. Her company, Madame C.J. ordered, must always be run by women.

The Bottom Line

In January 1998, the United States Postal Service issued a new 32-cent stamp in honor of Madame C.J. Walker. A'Lelia Bundles, her great-great-granddaughter, joined Postal Service officials in paying tribute to the cosmetics tycoon. Bundles often quotes Madame C.J.'s own words. Speaking to the National Negro Business League in 1912, Madame C.J. said,

> I am a woman who came from the fields of the South. I was promoted from there to the

Teacher Roberta Stickney (left) and postmaster Joe Santana show off the Black Heritage stamp that honors Madame C.J. Walker in Stickney's classroom in Gardena, California.

washtub. Then I was promoted to the cook kitchen, and from there I promoted myself into the business of manufacturing hair goods and preparations. I have built my own factory on my own ground.[3]

Had she been present to admire her stamp, Madame C.J. might have repeated another strong statement.

If I have accomplished anything in life it is because I have been willing to work hard. . . . I have always believed in keeping at things with a vim. There is no royal flower-strewn road to success, . . . for what success I have obtained is the result of many sleepless nights and real hard work.[4]

The symbol of Madame C.J.'s success, the Villa Lewaro, has become a national historic landmark. The one-time laundress would be pleased. She once said she hoped that her home would stand as a monument to "what a lone woman had accomplished."[5] If visitors find it hard to believe that most African-American women once toiled as servants and field hands, Madame C.J. would set the record straight. "I had to make my own living and my own opportunity!" she once said. "But I made it! That's why I want to say . . . don't sit down and wait for the opportunities to come. . . . Get up and make them!"[6]

7

Louis B. Mayer

Movie Tycoon

In the 1930s and early 1940s, a night out at the movies was a big event for Americans. Tickets were cheap, and movies provided thrills, laughs, and romance. Many of the most popular films came from Metro-Goldwyn-Mayer (MGM), the world's largest film studio. The "Mayer" of MGM was movie tycoon Louis B. Mayer.

Mayer had a special fondness for low-budget, high-profit B films. His favorites were the Andy Hardy films, a series of fourteen movies produced between 1937 and 1943. Teenager Andy Hardy, played by Mickey Rooney, lived with his family in a fictional town in Idaho. Judy Garland played the pretty girl next door. Each script filled the screen with comedy, music, youthful high spirits, and a touch of drama.

Louis B. Mayer (1885–1957)

The Andy Hardy films reflected Mayer's love of American family values. Always alert to anything that trashed those values, he watched each new Andy Hardy film in its rough cut. If he disliked a scene, he ordered the director to reshoot it. In one film Mayer went so far as to write a prayer for Andy Hardy to recite. "Dear God," the prayer says, "Please don't let my Mom die . . . she's the best Mom in the world. Thank you, God." To his writers, he said, "Let's see you beat that for a prayer!" Mayer also warned the writers, "Don't try to make these films any better. Keep them just the way they are."[1]

Starting Out

Many details of Louis B. Mayer's early life are uncertain. *Current Biography* says that Lazar Mayer (his name at birth) was born near Minsk in Russia. Other writers place his birth in Lithuania.[2] As a young man wishing to appear older, Mayer gave his birth date as 1882. Later he moved it up to 1885. Even the day was doubtful, so he picked July 4—the ideal American birthday. His parents changed his name to Louis when they settled in Canada in the late 1880s.

Prejudice against Jews had driven Jacob and Sarah Mayer out of Russia. With five lively children in tow, they settled in the New Brunswick town of St. John. Jacob made his living by peddling scrap. Legend says that Louis dropped out of school at twelve to help his father. But, in fact, he stayed in school and graduated in 1902.[3]

Louis moved to Boston in 1904 and set up his own junk business. Five months later he married Margaret Shenberg. On the marriage license he added a middle initial to make his name sound more dignified. Later, he told friends that the *B* stood for Burton. In the years that followed, the couple welcomed two daughters, Edith and Irene.

At that time a new craze was sweeping the country. Americans flocked to theaters called nickelodeons to watch motion-picture films. In 1907, Louis borrowed six hundred dollars and bought a grimy theater in Haverhill, Massachusetts. He fixed it up, changed its name to the Orpheum, and announced that he would show only the finest films. Customers soon filled the seats, and Louis was ready to expand.

By 1914, Louis owned the largest theater chain in New England. That was the year he cleared a huge profit by distributing *Birth of a Nation*. He did not worry that the film's treatment of African Americans increased the nation's racial tensions. By that time, his contacts with filmmaking had convinced him that producers made more money and had more fun than did theater owners. It was time, Louis told himself, to finance and supervise the making of his own films.

Fame and Fortune

Louis B. Mayer produced his first film, *Virtuous Wives*, in 1918. Like most of his later films, it told a good story, starred a beautiful actress, and was very well-made. Later that year, Mayer moved his company to California, the heart of the movie business. Soon he was hard at work on a new film. Filmed largely on the local beaches, *A Midnight Romance* was ready for screening by the end of the year.

Now that he was a producer, Mayer had to line up theater owners to show his films. A deal with First National Exhibitors' Circuit took care of that problem. Next, he needed someone to bankroll his filmmaking. That piece fell into place when Marcus Loew, owner of Metro Pictures, signed Mayer to produce four pictures a year.

In 1922, Mayer met Irving Thalberg, head of production for Universal Studio. Mayer recognized the younger man's talent as a filmmaker and hired him as vice-president of Louis B. Mayer Pictures. Until disputes over money drove a wedge between them, he looked on Thalberg as the son he never had.

In 1923, Metro Pictures took over the vast Goldwyn Studio. When Loew looked around for someone to run it, a friend suggested Louis B. Mayer. After some hard bargaining, Mayer agreed to merge his company with Metro-Goldwyn. As general manager of Metro-Goldwyn-Mayer, he drew a salary of $1,500 a week. Thalberg signed on at $650 a week to handle the artistic end of the business. MGM's roster grew to include silent-film greats Buster Keaton, Lillian Gish, Greta Garbo, and Lon Chaney.

Ben Hur, a film about Christians struggling to survive in ancient Rome, was filming in Italy when

Mayer took charge. The new boss looked at the scenes already filmed and saw a disaster in the making. Moving swiftly, Mayer replaced the director, writer, and leading man. That improved matters, but filming still dragged. The only spectacular thing about *Ben Hur*, Mayer complained, was its $2 million cost.[4] To salvage what he could, he moved the production to California. At MGM, crews built a Roman arena, and daredevil actors staged the great chariot race. A year later, in 1925, *Ben Hur* opened to cheers from filmgoers and critics alike.

Ben Hur was Louis B. Mayer's first blockbuster success as head of Metro-Goldwyn-Mayer studios. Ramon Navarro (pictured) was Mayer's choice to replace the original leading man.

Before long, MGM was turning out a feature film each week. Behind the studio's high white walls, Mayer ruled his kingdom from a three-story office building. He seemed to be everywhere at once. Short and thick-chested, he stared down Hollywood's "beautiful people" with his keen dark eyes. Foes called him a ruthless, quick-tempered tyrant. Friends admired his love of hard work, his grasp of filmmaking, and his devotion to MGM. That feeling carried over to his treatment of his employees. They were expected to think of him as a stern but loving father.[5]

Sound was added to films in the late 1920s. When some of his actors could not make the switch to the "talkies," Mayer developed fresh stars. Joan Crawford, Jean Harlow, Clark Gable, Robert Montgomery, William Powell, and Norma Shearer emerged as America's new heartthrobs. In 1927, in an effort to bring peace to warring producers, writers, actors, and directors, Mayer helped found the Academy of Motion Picture Arts and Sciences. Today the Academy is best known for awarding the Oscars to each year's top films and filmmakers.

Mayer's three thousand dollar a week salary was dwarfed by his share of MGM's profits. By 1937 he was earning $1.3 million a year. That income made him the nation's best paid executive, an honor he held for nine years. His 1939 hit, *The Wizard of Oz,* further enriched Mayer and his studio. Never one to waste money, he paid the midgets who played the Munchkins less than he paid the dog that played Toto.[6]

Mayer and his wife had grown apart, and they divorced in 1944. He found a new companion in Lorena Danker and married her a few years later. Bigger problems, however, were waiting at the studio. After World War II, Mayer failed to adjust as people moved to the suburbs and stayed home to watch television. The studios lost another source of profits when they were forced to sell their theater chains. MGM's $18 million profit in 1946 turned into a $6.5 million loss in 1948. Despite the loss, Mayer refused to cut back on the studio's lavish production budgets.

Dore Schary took over as production boss, but Mayer would not stop meddling. Finally, Mayer told his boss, Nicholas Schenk of Loew's, to choose between him and his younger rival. When Schenk called his bluff and chose Schary, Mayer walked out. His resignation in 1951 ended a twenty-seven-year run at MGM.

The aging filmmaker tried to start over with a wide-screen process called Cinerama. The old Mayer magic worked for a time, but the novelty wore off and ticket sales slumped. Mayer then spent two years in a futile attempt to start a stockholders' rebellion against his old friends at Loew's. By then he was fighting another losing battle—this time against leukemia. Mayer died, confused and depressed, on October 29, 1957.

The Bottom Line

The film industry breeds tycoons—and Louis B. Mayer once stood head and shoulders above the rest. From his white-carpeted office at MGM, he ruled over the largest pool of creative talent in the film industry. An army of technicians, directors, actors, and writers worked for him, and Mayer used them shrewdly. No detail escaped his sharp eye, and he seemed to know exactly what the public wanted.

Mayer often arranged "deals" with producers who needed MGM's stars for their films. By loaning Clark Gable to David O. Selznick for *Gone With the Wind*, he gained the rights to distribute the block-buster film when it came out in 1939. His rivals hated him for driving hard bargains, but they had to admit that he was the best at what he did.

Mayer often went out of his way to help employees who had problems. In return, he demanded total loyalty. When it came to contracts, he knew how to play on the vanities of his talent. As writer Herman Mankiewicz noted, "He had the memory of an elephant and the hide of an elephant. The only difference is that elephants are vegetarians and Mayer's diet was his fellow man."

"I want to rule by love, not by fear," the showman said in his own defense.[7] Rule he did, though not always by love. His great tragedy, however, was that he outlived the era he had done so much to create. Hollywood's Golden Age died nearly ten years before Louis B. Mayer breathed his last.

John H. Johnson (1918–   )

John H. Johnson

Publishing Tycoon

John H. Johnson was not content with his reign as a publishing tycoon. That was an old story, one that had begun thirty years earlier. Now it was 1973 and people were saying he was too tired and too rich to take on a new challenge. Johnson told himself that the rules that had guided his career would work in a new field. The challenge, he decided, lay in women's cosmetics.

Johnson had watched his *Ebony* magazine models as they mixed cosmetics suited to their dark skin tones. Now, certain he had spotted a market, he went to the top cosmetics firms. One by one, each refused to produce a line aimed at African-American women. Angry at what appeared to be racism, Johnson took his samples to a private lab. A chemist analyzed the lotions and worked out a way to duplicate them. The models loved the samples the lab mixed up and asked for more.

Good results did not guarantee success. Department store buyers worried that white customers would stay away if they stocked Johnson's Fashion Fair line. Locked out of major markets, the new venture lost a million dollars a year for five years. Instead of giving up, Johnson began calling on the heads of the big department store chains. Using sales techniques polished by his years in publishing, he opened one chain after another. Sales took off, and today Fashion Fair cosmetics sell briskly in the United States, Canada, and Africa.

As Johnson tells it, "I have a lifetime of experience in changing nos to yeses. . . . I sell for the sheer joy of selling."[1]

Starting Out

Johnny Johnson was born on January 19, 1918, in Arkansas City, Arkansas. Leroy and Gertrude Johnson were poor, but they taught their children the values of honesty and hard work. Leroy died in a sawmill accident when Johnny was six. Gertrude went on cooking for white families, and took a switch to her son when he misbehaved.

Johnny's schooling nearly ended with the eighth grade because the local high school did not admit African Americans. A new life opened up when

Gertrude moved Johnny and his half sister, Beulah, to Chicago in 1933. Gertrude, now married to James Williams, was drawn by the promise of better jobs and better schools. Johnny enrolled at Wendell Phillips High, where his classmates laughed at his down-home ways. He silenced the taunts by studying hard and polishing his speaking skills.

Hard times closed in as the country sank into the Great Depression. James could not find work, and Gertrude and Beulah lost their jobs. Gertrude applied for welfare, but the city turned her down. She wrote to President Franklin D. Roosevelt and a reply from the White House helped change the minds of city officials. For three years, the family survived on the city's monthly food handouts.

Johnny took pride in his work as editor of the school paper. The hours he spent working on the *Phillipsite* directed him toward a career in journalism. At graduation in 1936, he listed his name as John Harold Johnson. A teacher had convinced him it sounded more dignified that way.

The honor graduate met Harry Pace, president of Supreme Liberty Life Insurance, at a luncheon. Pace, impressed by the bright young man, asked about his college plans. John explained that college would have to wait until he saved some money. Pace gave him a part-time job, which allowed John to attend the University of Chicago.

Fame and Fortune

Johnson went to work for Supreme Liberty Life in September 1936. After two years of on-the-job training, Pace asked his protégé to serve as his assistant. Johnson dropped out of college to focus on his new job. He later said, "My real school from 1936 to 1941 was the university of Supreme Life."[2] One lesson he learned was that a business could prosper by serving the African-American community.

Pace put Johnson in charge of the firm's newspaper. It was a stroke of luck for a young man who dreamed of being a journalist. As editor, Johnson learned to focus on the tasks at hand. He also learned that he had to double-check to make sure that staffers followed through on assignments. To better understand the insurance business, he learned how to sell policies door-to-door.

In 1940, Johnson was making enough money to buy his first car. He also fell in love with graduate student Eunice Walker, and they married the following year. Unable to have children of their own, they adopted two babies. John, Jr., died at age twenty-five from sickle-cell anemia. Linda Johnson Rice grew up to become chief executive officer (CEO) of her father's publishing company.

Pace gave Johnson an assignment in 1942 that changed the young man's life. The new task was to prepare a weekly digest of events involving African Americans. When friends badgered him for copies,

Johnson guessed he was standing on a gold mine. Why not publish a magazine for African Americans based on the wildly successful *Reader's Digest* model? Johnson took the idea to publishers, but they all gave him the brush-off. Rather than give up, he vowed to publish the magazine himself.

Johnson first borrowed five hundred dollars, using his mother's furniture as a pledge of repayment. He spent the money on a mailing of twenty thousand flyers to Supreme Life customers. The flyers announced the birth of *Negro Digest* and asked for a two-dollar prepaid subscription. To Johnson's delight, the mailing brought in three thousand orders. In November 1942, the first five thousand copies rolled off the presses.

Johnson took his magazine to local distributors and asked them to sell it. When they refused, he sent thirty friends from store to store to ask for *Negro Digest*. After a distributor heard the message and ordered five hundred copies, Johnson gave his friends the money to buy every copy. Now the word was out, and buyers scooped up copies from newsstand shelves. The first press run sold out, and a second press run sold out almost as quickly.

Johnson was not called into the Army during World War II. The government kept him where he was because his magazine built support for the war effort among African Americans. In November 1945, with the war over and sales soaring, Johnson launched *Ebony*. The new publication was a lively picture magazine filled with positive images of African-American life. The first press run of twenty-five thousand copies sold out.

Johnson's next task was to build *Ebony's* circulation. He breathed more easily at the end of the first year when sales reached nearly half a million copies per issue. With those numbers in hand, Johnson set about selling the big-name ads that *Ebony* needed to survive. After the national advertising agencies turned him down, he began calling on corporate CEOs. The breakthrough came when Eugene McDonald of Zenith agreed to advertise in *Ebony*. Better still, McDonald urged his fellow CEOs to follow his lead.

In 1951, alert to new trends, Johnson replaced *Negro Digest* with the pocket-size *Jet. Negro Digest* returned in 1961 as *Black World.* The new magazine featured the work of the best African-American writers and poets. *EM,* aimed at African-American men, arrived later. All are produced in a modern eleven-story office building in the heart of Chicago's Loop.

Neither fame nor fortune has gone to Johnson's head. Drawing on childhood lessons, he does not smoke or drink, and he prefers work to vacations. Those who meet him come away impressed by his charm, energy, and devotion to African-American causes. Observers also glimpse a man who keeps tight control of everything that goes on in his company. His workers know he will pay their hospital bills—and fire them if they don't produce.[3]

Johnson shows few signs of slowing down. He advises presidents, sits on the boards of major corporations, and speaks to college students and civic groups. Along with Fashion Fair cosmetics, his interests include radio stations and his old employer, Supreme Life. His success, he notes, proves that African Americans can climb to the top of the business ladder.

The Bottom Line

John H. Johnson's success story is a classic American tale. He was raised in poverty but refused to stay poor. Time and again he had to fight racial prejudice as he built his publishing empire. He was never trained in sales, but he raised selling to a fine art.

In his 1989 book, *Succeeding Against the Odds*, Johnson wrote about the money he's made and the honors he's received. One high point came in 1982, when *Forbes* magazine named him to its list of the four hundred richest Americans. The report said he was worth $150 million, a number Johnson does not dispute. "Whatever the correct figure," he says, "I earned it, and I'm still earning it. I work harder today than I did when I started out. . . . In fact, if I were young again, . . . I could be even more successful."[4]

Johnson takes an equal pride in the honors that have come his way. The college dropout receives honorary degrees almost yearly. He's been named Chicagoan of the Year, the first African American to receive that award. Junior Achievement voted him

John H. Johnson, a popular inspirational speaker, wears cap and gown for a speech to the Class of 1996 at the University of Southern California in Los Angeles.

into its Business Hall of Fame. Even Arkansas City rolled out the red carpet when he came home for a visit.

Ask Johnson for the secret of his success, and he has a ready reply. "Hard work, dedication, and perseverance will overcome almost any prejudice and open almost any door," he says. "And if my life has meaning . . . it is because millions of Americans, Black and White, have proved through me that the [American] Dream is still alive and well and working in America."[5]

9

An Wang

Technology Tycoon

An Wang's English was far from perfect, but he possessed a world-class brain. In 1948, the Chinese immigrant earned his doctorate in applied physics and went to work at the Harvard Computation Laboratory. This was the dawn of the computer age. At the lab, a boxcar-sized computer used mechanical switches to store and retrieve data. The lab's boss, Dr. Howard Aiken, asked Wang to figure out a way to use magnetism to replace the noisy switches.

Once a metal is magnetized by a flow of current, Wang knew, it holds that "on" state. Reverse the current's flow and the metal reverts to its "off" state. In a computer, that process can be used to "read" the bit of stored data. The reading process, however, also erases the data bit.

An Wang (1920–1990)

Wang designed tiny doughnut-shaped magnets to store his data. Then he sent different kinds of currents through these memory cores. The cores worked well except that reading the data also erased it. He began to despair of finding a solution. "[O]ne day while I was walking through Harvard Yard, an idea came to me in a flash," Wang said. Erasing the data didn't matter, because "I could simply rewrite the data immediately afterward." The entire cycle would take only a few thousandths of a second![1]

Before long, Wang had linked a series of nickel-iron "doughnuts" into a fast, reliable memory system. Sensing the value of his invention, he applied for a patent. The stage was set for the explosive growth of the computer industry.

Starting Out

An Wang (his name means "Peaceful King") was born in Shanghai, China, on February 7, 1920. He was the second of five children. In those years China was being torn apart by civil war. The family escaped the turmoil of Shanghai by moving thirty miles up the Yangtze River to the town of Kun San.

An's father, Yin-lu Wang, taught at a school that did not offer first or second grade. As a result, six-year-old An was thrown into the third grade. The boy struggled at first, but soon found that he could keep up with his older classmates. He excelled in science and math, but lagged behind in social studies. Fourth grade brought the challenge of English lessons. Thanks to his father, An had studied the language since he was four.

An had to take a tough exam to qualify for junior high school. He surprised his parents by earning the highest scores of any child who took the test. After junior high he went on to Shanghai Provincial High. The thirteen-year-old made friends by playing soccer and table tennis. From there he moved on to study electrical engineering at Chaio Tung University in Shanghai. His high entry marks earned him the post of class president.

War between Japan and China broke out in 1937. To escape the fighting, the school relocated to a neutral zone set up by European nations. An graduated in 1940 and contributed to China's war effort. Because of his training, he was asked to head up a group of student engineers who made radio sets for the army.

Wang's fine work earned him a trip to the United States for further study. In 1945, he said good-bye to his young wife and made the long journey to the West. At Harvard, he found that the principles of science are the same the world over. On the strength of grades that were mostly A's and A+'s, An received a master's degree in 1946 and a doctorate in 1948.

Fame and Fortune

All through his student days, An Wang planned to return home to China. He changed his mind after the Communists came to power in his homeland. By this time both his parents were dead, and his Chinese wife had divorced him. He marked the start of his new life by marrying Lorraine Chiu in 1949. The happy marriage produced three children—sons Fred and Courtney and daughter Juliette.

In 1951, Wang left Harvard and started his own business. Working out of a small office, he sold memory cores to research labs. In his sales pitch he billed his operation as Wang Laboratories. At first, he felt it was a big day if he sold four handmade memory

Thanks to the work of Dr. An Wang and his fellow scientists, today's desktop computers are smaller, faster, and more powerful than the room-sized Univac of the 1940s (pictured).

cores at four dollars each. To make ends meet, he lectured at Northeastern University and did consulting work. Wang also designed and sold digital counting devices. Although the lab took in only $3,253.60 for the last half of 1951, Wang knew he was on the right track.

Four years later, Wang received the patent for his memory cores. The year 1955 was memorable in other ways as well. The Wangs became American citizens and purchased a ten-room home in a Boston suburb. Wang also turned his growing company into a family-owned corporation.

A year later, giant IBM bought Wang's memory core patent for four hundred thousand dollars. The inventor later complained that IBM used unfair tactics to keep the price down. The money arrived about the time the first transistors hit the market. Wang put the tiny devices to work in a line of hot-selling automated control units.

The road was rocky at times. In 1959, to raise capital for expansion, Wang sold a quarter of his business for fifty thousand dollars. Within a few years the lucky purchaser's share was worth $100 million. In another venture, Wang developed and built a fast typesetting machine for Compugraphic. Just as Wang's sales passed $1 million for the first time, Compugraphic broke the partnership. The company told him it was going to build the machines itself.

Wang swallowed hard and went back to work. Sensing a growing demand for small calculators, he introduced the LOCI in 1965. Unlike other calculators of the day, the user-friendly LOCI fit easily on a desk. The price was a hefty sixty-five hundred dollars, but research labs around the world lined up to place orders. As rivals brought out cheaper calculators, Wang stayed ahead by designing more advanced machines.

The Doctor, as his workers called him, always wore a gray suit and a bow tie. If he was forced to discipline someone, his full, oval face looked more sorrowful than angry. Brainy and self-confident, he went through his days jotting down ideas on scraps of paper. Lorraine always saved the scribbled drawings and notes she found in his pockets.[2]

Wang took his company public in 1967. Brokers offered 240,000 shares at $12.50 a share. By the end of the first day of trading, the price had soared to $40.50. Because employees had been allowed to buy in at $4.17 a share, many made small fortunes. Wang's secretary, who owned a hundred shares, danced around and shouted, "I'm rich, I'm rich!"[3]

In the late 1960s, calculator prices fell as integrated circuits made their appearance. Wang met the test by shifting to computers. The challenges were immense, but the company began shipping the Wang 2200 in 1972. It turned out to be the Volkswagen of small computer systems. Customers liked the 2200's ease of use, and the fact that Wang kept improving it. Even today, a third of the sixty-five thousand Wangs sold in the 1970s are still running.

In 1976, Wang changed gears again and introduced a user-friendly word processor. Typists loved the speed with which they could enter and edit text displayed on a screen. Big corporations deserted IBM and rushed to buy from Wang, even though a fully loaded Wang WPS sold for thirty thousand dollars. The Doctor shared his success by giving his workers generous stock options.

Wang retired from day-to-day management in 1983. In 1976, he had predicted that his company would reach a billion dollars in sales within ten years. For once he was wrong—in 1986 sales passed the $3 billion mark. From that high point, with the Doctor in semiretirement, the company began to slide. Its word processors could not match the power of the desktop computers produced by IBM and Apple.

An Wang died of throat cancer in 1990. Two years later his company filed for bankruptcy. From that low point, Wang Laboratories overhauled itself and regained its footing. The Doctor would not have been content with anything less.

The Bottom Line

In his autobiography, An Wang wrote,

> My education, my research at the Harvard Computational Laboratory, and my career, starting and building Wang Laboratories, have all been enormous fun. My days are spent doing the

things I really want to do. The satisfaction of turning an idea into something real never diminishes, and the great gift of change is that it continually replenishes the stock of new ideas that might be brought to life. The thrill of this challenge more than compensates for the setbacks that are the price of learning and growth. There are still many lessons to be learned.[4]

Wang knew the United States had been good to him. Like Andrew Carnegie, a fellow immigrant, he tried to give something back. Drawing on a fortune of some $1.6 billion, the Doctor gave $4 million to save Boston's decaying Performing Arts Center. A grateful city renamed it the Wang Center for Performing Arts. Wang also gave large gifts to support education. His favorite project was the Wang Institute of Graduate Studies. He spent millions to create a center where top scientists can gather to study software engineering and Chinese culture.

Wherever engineers gather, they still talk about Dr. An Wang. Some marvel at his forty-four patents, others wonder at his ability to foresee advances in technology. If he made a mistake, "he had the wisdom and vision to perceive it quickly and correct his course."[5]

Wang described his management style in these words: "You don't need special training to learn how to run a business," he said. "What you do need is the ability to observe, to test your theories in practice, and to learn from your mistakes."[6]

William Henry Gates III (1955–   )

Bill Gates

Computer Software Tycoon

In 1980, Bill Gates received a phone call that helped shape the Information Age. At twenty-five, Gates was a Harvard dropout and self-described computer nerd. He and his friend Paul Allen believed that the personal computer was destined to find a home on desktops everywhere. They had founded Microsoft in 1975 to provide software for those computers. These were pioneer days, and Gates had a head start on the field. While still in college he had written a programming language called BASIC (Basic All-Purpose Symbolic Instruction Code) for the first microcomputer, the Altair 8800.

The phone call came from IBM. The giant computer firm wanted to use Microsoft BASIC in its new personal computer. After several secret meetings,

IBM and Microsoft struck a bigger deal. In addition to BASIC, Gates agreed to create a new operating system (OS). Called MS-DOS (for Microsoft Disc Operating System), the operating system software translated the user's commands into language the computer could understand.

Faced with tight deadlines, Gates and Allen went shopping. They found an OS they liked at Seattle Computer Products. By working day and night Gates and his programmers rewrote SCP's QDOS to make it run on IBM's machine.[1]

Gates then proved he was a business genius, too. MS-DOS, he said, belonged to Microsoft. Any computer maker could use his program—but they would have to pay a licensing fee. Ten years later, Gates followed the same strategy when he grafted the user-friendly *Windows* OS onto MS-DOS. By the 1990s, the young software tycoon's programs were running 90 percent of the world's computers.

Getting Started

William Henry Gates III was born in Seattle, Washington, on October 28, 1955. He was the second of William and Mary Gates's three children. Both parents were active in the community, and they raised their children to follow their example. At home, the family often played cards and board games with a passion. "Winning mattered," Bill's lawyer father recalls.[2]

Bill earned top marks in math and science when he started school. Shy and small for his age, he fared less well on the playground. In 1968 his parents sent him to Lakeside School, a private school that stressed bookwork. Bill met Paul Allen there, and the two friends explored the brave new world of computers together. Within the first few months of their eighth-grade year, they used up the school's yearly computer budget.

Bill, Paul, and two friends formed the Lakeside Programmers Group. To test their skills, the boys made a deal with Computer Center Corporation (CCC) to fix the "bugs" in their system. In return, CCC gave the young programmers all the computer time they wanted. Bill used his hours to teach himself several computer languages.

In 1970, Lakeside paid the boys twenty-four hundred dollars to schedule students into classes. Bill and Paul wrote a program that did the job—and put Bill in classes with the school's cutest girls. Next, the boys started a company called Traf-O-Data. The small computers they designed measured traffic flow on city streets. Sales of the device topped twenty thousand dollars in 1972–1973.

Bill spent part of his senior year debugging a computer system for a defense contractor. That fall, torn between computers and a career as a lawyer, he enrolled at Harvard. Before long he was staying up late to write his BASIC program for the Altair. In April 1975, at Paul's urging, Gates dropped out and moved to Albuquerque, New Mexico. Microsoft was up and running.

Fame and Fortune

Microsoft racked up its first million dollars in sales in 1978. At that point Allen talked his partner into moving back to Seattle. He wanted to see water and trees again, he said. Gates, who missed water-skiing, agreed.[3] The partners also felt the move would lead to further growth. They were right. Microsoft doubled in size every year for the next five years.

Gates hired bright, high-energy programmers fresh out of school. Later, he explained his formula. "Pick good people, use small teams, give them excellent tools . . . so they are very productive in terms of what they are doing," he said. "Make it very clear that they can change the spec[ifications]. Make them feel like they are very much in control."[4] He pushed his people to work sixty-hour weeks—and supplied them with free Coca-Cola.

With MS-DOS selling well, Gates moved Microsoft into word processing. The result was Microsoft *Word*. Older programs forced users to memorize complex keyboard commands. *Word* users clicked on simple menus and could see what their pages would look like when printed. Users also enjoyed the freedom of moving the cursor around the screen with a mouse. Thanks to *Word*, the small pointing devices became a standard part of the computer scene.

Allen left in 1983, a victim of overwork and Hodgkin's disease. Gates kept on going, and by 1986 he had moved Microsoft into a wooded setting in Redmond, Washington. The company was growing fast, thanks in large measure to *Windows.* Computer nerds loved DOS, but using commands like *C> COPY TYCOON.DOC A:* to copy a file to a floppy disk annoyed most users. *Windows* changed all that by allowing people to access programs easily. In 1988, Gates added multitasking (the ability to run several programs at once). Further advances came with *Windows 3.x, Windows NT, Windows 95, Windows CE, Windows 98,* and *Windows 2000.*

One of Microsoft's few missteps could have doomed the company. All through the early 1990s, Gates ignored the growth of the Internet. When he woke up to the threat posed by fast-growing Netscape, he rallied his troops. Microsoft programmers dragged their sleeping bags to the office and went to work. A few months later, Gates announced that his Internet browser was ready to go.

Gates took his company public in 1986. The sale of Microsoft stock made him an instant billionaire. In 1998, his holdings were said to be worth some $50 billion. As Microsoft grew, software companies stung by the company's success began to sue Gates for unfair business practices. With the aid of well-paid lawyers, he has won most of those battles.

The government joined the hunt by looking into charges that Gates was breaking antitrust laws.

Despite the headlines, the agreements that installed Windows on most new computers did not change. In 1998, the Justice Department and twenty states filed antitrust lawsuits against Microsoft. Gates ran full-page ads in the newspapers to argue that the case was "a step backward . . . for the personal computer industry." Experts looked at both sides and predicted that the case would drag on for years.

Gates is a workaholic, but he does have a life outside the office. In 1994, he gave up his bachelor ways and married Melinda French. Their daughter, Jennifer Katherine, was born two years later. In 1997 the couple moved into a new home on Lake Washington. The $40 million, forty-thousand-square-foot structure features three glass-walled pavilions, a thirty-car garage, and a trout stream. As visitors wander through the house, they are greeted with a variety of pictures, music, and movies.

Gates, still full of energy in his mid-forties, says he will devote ten more years to Microsoft. Then, taking a page from Andrew Carnegie's book, he promises to spend his money on good causes. As a first step toward fulfilling that vow, he has established a $200 million foundation. If his past record is any guide, much of the money will go to colleges and libraries. When he retires, Gates looks forward to pushing a program that installs computers in inner-city schools.

What kind of person is this immensely wealthy man? Friends agree that he's the smartest guy they've ever met. If he is at his desk, he keeps two computers busy. On one screen he studies streams of data from the Internet. On the other he handles hundreds of e-mail messages. Gates is shy with strangers, but when he relaxes, he is a good listener and a fine storyteller. He loves fast cars, and he has taken up golf in recent years. Most of all, despite his youth, he is a skilled, confident tycoon. One writer describes him as "a technologist turned entrepreneur," the perfect symbol of the Information Age.[5]

The Bottom Line

During their school days, Paul Allen once took on a programming job without his younger friend. When he saw that he needed Gates's coding skills, he called for help. "O.K., but I'm in charge," Gates told him, "and I'll get used to being in charge, and it'll be hard to deal with me from now on unless I'm in charge."[6] Everyone who knows Gates agrees with the truth of that statement.

In the years that have followed, Gates has transformed the computer world. Microsoft programs, ranging from Windows and Word to Flight Simulator and Encarta, have become household names. Gates says he won't be satisfied until *every* household has its own computer. And if he has his way, all those computers will be running the newest version of Windows.

Microsoft's success has created wealth and power for its founder, but it has created problems, too. The

Gates now oversees the Microsoft campus in Redmond, Washington. In 1998, the value of his company holdings gave him the title of "America's richest person" for the fifth year in a row.

decision to couple the company's Internet browser with Windows 98, for example, led to a number of lawsuits. Also of concern to smaller companies is the fact that Microsoft's product line doesn't stop with Windows. Gates has watched his programs gain a dominant share of the market in such fields as word processing, desktop publishing, spreadsheets, and financial management.

Gates refuses to worry. He prefers to plan for a future where change will be the only constant. "We've only come a small way," he says,

> We haven't changed the way that markets are organized. We haven't changed the way people educate themselves, or socialize, or express their political opinions, in nearly the way we will over the next ten years. And so the software is going to have to lead the way and provide the kind of ease of use, security, and richness that these applications demand.[7]

Chapter Notes

Chapter 1. Cornelius Vanderbilt: Transportation Tycoon

1. Jerry E. Patterson, *The Vanderbilts* (New York: Harry N. Abrams, 1989), p. 38.

2. Arthur T. Vanderbilt II, *Fortune's Children* (New York: William Morrow, 1989), pp. 6–7.

3. Ibid., pp. 9–10.

4. Ibid., p. 36.

5. Ibid., p. 27.

Chapter 2. Andrew Carnegie: Steel Tycoon

1. Public Broadcasting Service, "Scientific Philanthropy," *The American Experience: The Richest Man in the World: Andrew Carnegie*, 1998, <http://www.pbs.org/wgbh/pages/amex/carnegie/sci.html> (April 1, 1999).

2. Public Broadcasting Service, "A Library of Your Own," *The American Experience: The Richest Man in the World: Andrew Carnegie*, 1998, <http://www.pbs.org/wgbh/pages/amex/carnegie/library.html> (April 1, 1999).

3. Harold C. Livesay, *American Made: Men Who Shaped the American Economy* (Boston: Little, Brown, 1979), p. 99.

4. John Bowman, *Andrew Carnegie* (Englewood Cliffs, N.J.: Silver Burdett Press, 1989), p. 49.

5. Alvin F. Harlow, *Andrew Carnegie* (Chicago: Kingston House, 1959), p. 99.

6. Public Broadcasting Service, "The Wrong Career Path?" *The American Experience: The Richest Man in the World: Andrew Carnegie*, 1998, <http://www.pbs.org/wgbh/pages/amex/carnegie/wrongpath.html> (April 1, 1999).

7. Public Broadcasting Service, "The Carnegie Legacy," *The American Experience: The Richest Man in the World: Andrew Carnegie*, 1998, <http://www.pbs.org/wgbh/pages/amex/carnegie/legacy.html> (April 1, 1999).

8. Andrew Carnegie "The Gospel of Wealth," *North American Review*, vol. 148, June 1889, p. 664.

Chapter 3. John Pierpont (J.P.) Morgan: Financial Tycoon

1. Andrew Sinclair, *Corsair: The Life of J. Pierpont Morgan* (Boston: Little, Brown, 1981), p. 140.

2. George Wheeler, *Pierpont Morgan and Friends* (Englewood Cliffs, N.J.: Prentice-Hall, 1973), p. 257.

3. Bernard A. Weisberger, ed., *The Age of Steel and Steam* (New York: Time, 1964), p. 34.

4. Ibid., p. 177.

5. Sinclair, p. 126.

6. Weisberger, p. 14.

7. Ibid., p. 13.

8. Matthew Josephson, *The Robber Barons* (New York: Harcourt Brace, 1934), p. 441.

9. Wheeler, p. 1.

Chapter 4. John D. Rockefeller: Petroleum Tycoon

1. David Freeman Hawke, *John D.: The Founding Father of the Rockefellers* (New York: Harper & Row, 1980), p. 72.

2. Peter Collier and David Horowitz, *The Rockefellers* (New York: New American Library, 1976), p. 11.

3. Ibid., p. 17.

4. Hawke, p. 219.

Chapter 5. Henry Ford: Automobile Tycoon

1. Peter Collier and David Horowitz, *The Fords: An American Epic* (New York: Summit Books, 1987), pp. 40–41.

2. Ibid., p. 64.

3. David L. Lewis, *The Public Image of Henry Ford: An American Folk Hero and His Company* (Detroit: Wayne State University Press, 1976), pp. 69–77.

4. Collier and Horowitz, p. 96.

5. Ibid., p. 305.

6. Ibid., p. 189.

7. Ibid., p. 58.

8. Robert Locus, *Ford: The Man and the Machine* (Boston: Little, Brown, 1986), p. 238.

9. Collier and Horowitz, p. 13.

Chapter 6. Madame C.J. Walker: Cosmetics Tycoon

1. Jessie Carney Smith, ed., *Notable Black American Women* (Detroit: Gale Research, 1992), p. 1185.

2. *Los Angeles Times*, February 6, 1998, p. B3.

3. Smith, p. 1187.

4. Susan McHenry, *Madame C.J. Walker: Historic Entrepreneur*, <http://www.womenswire.com/watch/walker.html> (April 18, 1999).

5. Ibid.

6. Ibid.

Chapter 7. Louis B. Mayer: Movie Tycoon

1. Bosley Crowther, *Hollywood Rajah* (New York: Holt, Rinehart, & Winston, 1960), pp. 235–240.

2. "Louis B. Mayer," <http://www.mdle.com/classicfilms/BTC/prod10.htm> (April 18, 1999).

3. Charles Higham, *Merchant of Dreams: Louis B. Mayer, M.G.M., and the Secret Hollywood* (New York: Donald I. Fine Books, 1993), p. 12.

4. Samuel Marx, *Mayer and Thalberg: The Make-Believe Saints* (New York: Random House, 1975), p. 63.

5. Higham, p. 70.

6. Diana Altman, *Hollywood East: Louis B. Mayer and the Origins of the Studio System* (New York: Birch Lane Press, 1992), p. 219.

7. Ibid., p. 328.

Chapter 8. John H. Johnson: Publishing Tycoon

1. John H. Johnson [with Lerone Bennett, Jr.], *Succeeding Against the Odds* (New York: Warner Books, 1989), p. 345.

2. Ibid., pp. 87–88.

3. John A. Garraty, ed., *Encyclopedia of American Biography* (New York: HarperCollins, 1996), p. 618.

4. Johnson, p. 353.

5. Ibid., pp. 355–356.

Chapter 9. An Wang: Technology Tycoon

1. Dr. An Wang [with Eugene Linden], *Lessons: An Autobiography* (Reading, Mass.: Addison-Wesley, 1986), pp. 56–57.

2. Jim Hargrove, *Dr. An Wang: Computer Pioneer* (Chicago: Childrens Press, 1993), p. 53.

3. Wang, p. 150.

4. Ibid., p. 239.

5. Charles C. Kenney, *Riding the Runaway Horse: The Rise and Decline of Wang Laboratories* (Boston: Little, Brown, 1992), p. 119.

6. Wang, p. 221.

Chapter 10. Bill Gates: Computer Software Tycoon

1. Daniel Ichbiah and Susan L. Knepper, *The Making of Microsoft: How Bill Gates and His Team Created the World's Most Successful Software Company* (Rocklin, Calif.: Prima Publishing, 1991), pp. 78–79.

2. Walter Isaacson, "In Search of the Real Bill Gates," *Time*, January 13, 1997, p. 47.

3. Ichbiah and Knepper, p. 59.

4. David Allison, "Bill Gates Interview," *Smithsonian Institution*, 1996, <http://innovate.si.edu/history/gates/gates29.htm> (April 1, 1999).

5. Isaacson, p. 46.

6. Ibid., p. 48.

7. David Allison, "The 'Microsoft Way,'" *Smithsonian Institution*, 1996, <http://innovate.si.edu/history/gates/gates29.htm> (April 1, 1999).

Further Reading

Books

Boyd, Aaron. *Smart Money: The Story of Bill Gates.* Greensboro, N.C.: Morgan Reynolds, Inc., 1995.

Bundles, Alelia. *Madam C.J. Walker: Entrepreneur.* Bromall, Pa.: Chelsea House Publishers, 1991.

Dickinson, Joan D. *Bill Gates: Billionaire Computer Genius.* Springfield, N.J.: Enslow Publishers, Inc., 1997.

Hargrove, Jim. *Dr. An Wang: Computer Pioneer.* Danbury, Conn.: Children's Press, 1993.

Joseph, Paul. *Henry Ford.* Minneapolis: ABDO Publishing Company, 1996

Meltzer, Milton. *The Many Lives of Andrew Carnegie.* Danbury, Conn.: Franklin Watts, Inc., 1997.

Patterson, Jerry E. *The Vanderbilts.* New York: Harry N. Abrams, 1989.

Simon, Charnan. *Andrew Carnegie: Builder of Libraries.* Danbury, Conn.: Children's Press, 1998.

Shuker, Nancy. *John D. Rockefeller.* Parsippany, N.J.: Silver Burdett Press, 1989.

Strouse, Jean. *Morgan: American Financier.* New York: Random House, 1999.

Internet Addresses

Black Families.com—John H. Johnson: Education and Hard Work
<http://www.blackfamilies.com/business/family_finance/john_h_johnson.html>

The Film 100: Louis B. Mayer
<http://www.film100.com/cgi/direct.cgi?v.maye>

Index